Animal Top Tens

Asia's Most
Amazing Animals

Anita Ganeri

www.raintreepublishers.co.uk
Visit our website to find out more information about Raintree books.

To order:
☎ Phone 44 (0) 1865 888112
▤ Send a fax to 44 (0) 1865 314091
▢ Visit the Raintree Bookshop at www.raintreepublishers.co.uk to brows catalogue and order online

First published in Great Britain by Raintree,
Halley Court, Jordan Hill, Oxford OX2 8EJ,
part of Harcourt Education.
Raintree is a registered trademark of Harcourt
Education Ltd.

Editorial: Nancy Dickmann and Catherine Veitch
Design: Victoria Bevan and Geoff Ward
Illustrations: Geoff Ward
Picture Research: Mica Brancic
Production: Victoria Fitzgerald

Originated by Modern Age
Printed and bound by CTPS (China Translation
& Printing Services Ltd)

13-digit ISBN 978 1 4062 0915 0
12 11 10 09 08
10 9 8 7 6 5 4 3 2 1

British Library Cataloguing in Publication Data
Ganeri, Anita, 1961-
    Asia's Most Amazing Animals.
(Animal top tens)
    591.9'5
A full catalogue record for this book is available from
the British Library.

Acknowledgements
The author and publisher are grateful to the following
for permission to reproduce copyright material: ©Alamy
p. **12** (John Terence Turner); ©Ardea pp. **10** (Pascal
Goetgheluck), **20** (M. Watson), **27** (Tom & Pat Leeson);
©FLPA pp. **8**, **9** (Frans Lanting), **25** (Chris Mattison);
©FLPA/Foto Natura p. **26** (Konstantin Mikhailov);
©FLPA/Minden Pictures pp. **19** (Gerry Ellis), **21** (Colin
Monteath); ©FLPA/Minden Pictures/JH Editorial
p. **14** (Cyril Ruoso); ©Getty/National Geographic p. **13**
(Mattias Klum); ©Getty/Photographer's Choice p. **15**
(Theo Allofs); Naturepl p. **22** (Peter Scoones); ©NHPA
p. **23** (Karl Switak); ©OSF pp. **6** (Alan & Sandy Carey),
11, **24** (Juniors Bildarchiv); ©OSF/Digital Vision p. **4**;
©OSF/Earth Scenes/Animals Animals p. **17** (DANI/
JESKE N/A); ©OSF/Panorama Media (Beijing) Ltd
p. **16** (Weixiong Liu); ©OSF/PhotoDisc p. **18**
(Keren Su); ©OSF/Purestock p. **7**.

Cover photograph of a Bengal tiger, reproduced with
permission of PhotoLibrary/Corbis Corporation.

The publishers would like to thank Michael Bright for
his assistance with the preparation of this book.

Every effort has been made to contact copyright holders
of any material reproduced in this book. Any omissions
will be rectified in subsequent printings if notice is given
to the publishers.

Disclaimer
All the internet addresses (URLs) given in this book
were valid at time of going to press. However, due to
the dynamic nature of the Internet, some addresses may
have changed, or sites may have changed or ceased to
exist since publication. While the author and publishers
regret any inconvenience this may cause readers, no
responsibility for any such changes can be accepted by
either the author or the publishers. It is recommended
that adults supervise children on the Internet.

Contents

Some words are printed in bold, **like this**. You can find out what they mean on page 31 in the Glossary.

Asia

Asia is the world's largest continent. It covers almost 45,000,000 sq kilometres (17,370,000 sq miles). That is a third of the Earth's land surface. It stretches from Europe and Africa in the west to the Pacific Ocean in the east. The northern part of Asia lies in the icy Arctic. The southern part lies around the **equator** and is hot and steamy.

Asia is so enormous that it has many different kinds of landscape. There are giant mountain ranges and huge, empty **deserts**. There are also great lakes and long rivers. Away from the mainland, thousands of islands sit on either side of the equator.

Mt Gunung Bakur, in Indonesia, is one of many active volcanoes in Asia.

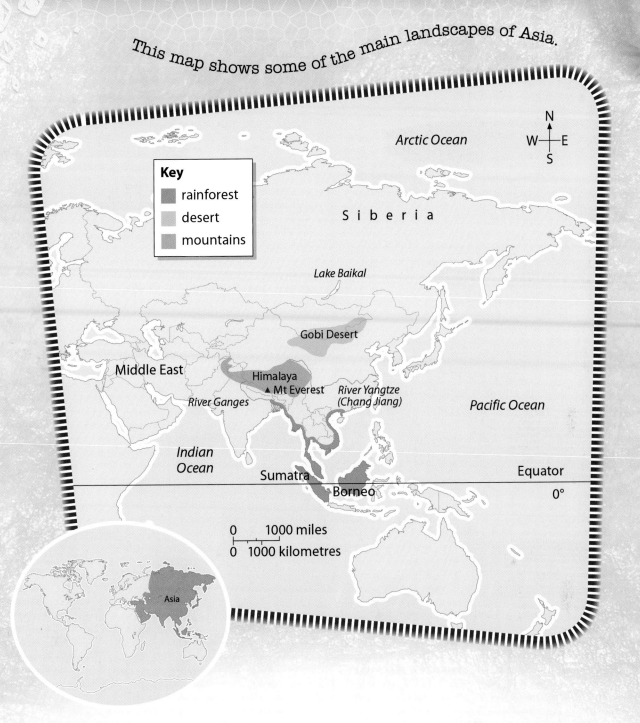

An amazing range of animals lives in these **habitats**. Bears and tigers live in the frozen north. Yaks and snow leopards make their homes on the windy mountain slopes. The forests are full of wildlife, from giant pandas to great apes. A few animals, such as camels, have even **adapted** to life in the scorching hot desert.

Bengal tiger

The Bengal tiger lives in India and Bangladesh. It needs a **habitat** with plenty of grass to hide behind when it hunts for food. It can live in woodlands, **rainforests**, and mangrove **swamps**.

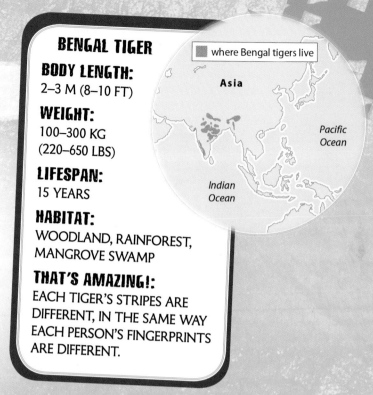

BENGAL TIGER

BODY LENGTH:
2–3 M (8–10 FT)

WEIGHT:
100–300 KG
(220–650 LBS)

LIFESPAN:
15 YEARS

HABITAT:
WOODLAND, RAINFOREST, MANGROVE SWAMP

THAT'S AMAZING!:
EACH TIGER'S STRIPES ARE DIFFERENT, IN THE SAME WAY EACH PERSON'S FINGERPRINTS ARE DIFFERENT.

where Bengal tigers live

Asia

Pacific Ocean

Indian Ocean

Bengal tiger cubs stay with their mother for two to three years.

A tiger eats as much as it can,
then hides the rest of its catch in the grass.

Tiger stripes
A tiger's coat is orange-brown with black stripes. This helps to **camouflage** the tiger as it stalks its prey. The stripes break up the tiger's outline as it lies in wait among the long grass.

Superb hunter

The tiger feeds on deer, buffalo, and wild pigs, which it hunts at night. Its body is built for catching and killing **prey**. The tiger silently stalks its prey until its victim is close by. Then it pounces. The tiger grabs its prey in its paws, which have sharp claws. It then kills its victim with a bite to the neck, using its long, pointed teeth.

Orang utan

The orang utan is a large ape with long red hair. It is only found on the islands of Sumatra and Borneo where it lives in the **rainforest**. It mostly feeds on fruit from rainforest trees, such as wild figs and mangoes. If there is not much fruit it will also eat leaves, seeds, and bark.

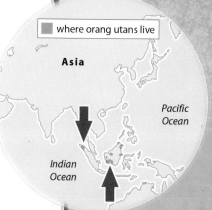

ORANG UTAN

BODY LENGTH:
1.3–1.8 M (4.2–5.9 FT)

WEIGHT:
35–80 KG (77–176 LBS)

LIFESPAN:
30–40 YEARS

HABITAT:
TROPICAL RAINFORESTS

THAT'S AMAZING!:
ORANG UTANS ARE ONE OF FOUR KINDS OF GREAT APES. THE OTHER THREE ARE GORILLAS, CHIMPANZEES, AND BONOBOS.

where orang utans live

Asia

Pacific Ocean

Indian Ocean

Male orang utans (like the one on the left) are about twice the size of females.

An orang utan swinging through the trees.

Life in the trees

Orang utans spend most of their time in the trees. They are well **adapted** to their forest life. They have long arms for swinging through the trees, and hook-shaped hands and feet for gripping branches. They use their strength to bend branches to make bridges between the gaps in the trees. At night they sleep in nests made from branches and twigs, high up in the trees.

Giant atlas moth

The giant atlas moth is one of the largest moths in the world. It lives in south-east Asia. The pattern on the moth's wings and the hooked wing tips help to scare off hungry **predators**. The wing tips look a bit like snakes' heads.

Male moths pick up the smell given off by a female moth with their long **antennae**.

Moth life cycle

Female moths attract males by giving off a strong smell. After **mating**, a female lays her eggs on a leaf. The eggs take about two weeks to hatch. The caterpillars feed on the plants around them, then spin silk cases around themselves. Inside, their bodies change into adults. An adult moth only lives for about two weeks while it mates, lays eggs, and dies.

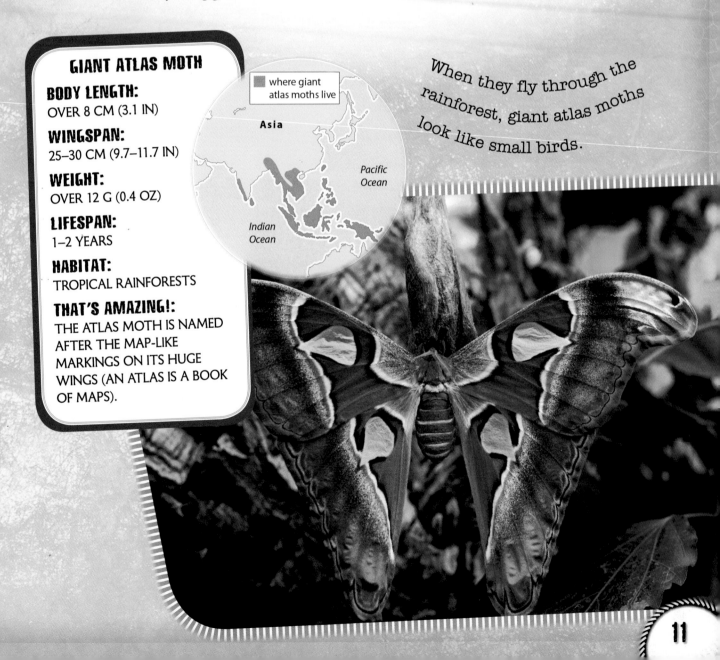

GIANT ATLAS MOTH

BODY LENGTH:
OVER 8 CM (3.1 IN)

WINGSPAN:
25–30 CM (9.7–11.7 IN)

WEIGHT:
OVER 12 G (0.4 OZ)

LIFESPAN:
1–2 YEARS

HABITAT:
TROPICAL RAINFORESTS

THAT'S AMAZING!:
THE ATLAS MOTH IS NAMED AFTER THE MAP-LIKE MARKINGS ON ITS HUGE WINGS (AN ATLAS IS A BOOK OF MAPS).

where giant atlas moths live

Asia

Pacific Ocean

Indian Ocean

When they fly through the rainforest, giant atlas moths look like small birds.

King cobra

The king cobra lives in the **rainforests** of India, southern China, and south-east Asia. It is the longest poisonous snake in the world. It is also one of the deadliest snakes.

As the cobra rears up, it gives a loud hiss which sounds like a dog growling.

Snake poison
A cobra's venom is made in sacs behind its eyes. When the cobra bites, the venom is injected through its long, hollow fangs. A cobra's venom stops its victim's heart and lungs working.

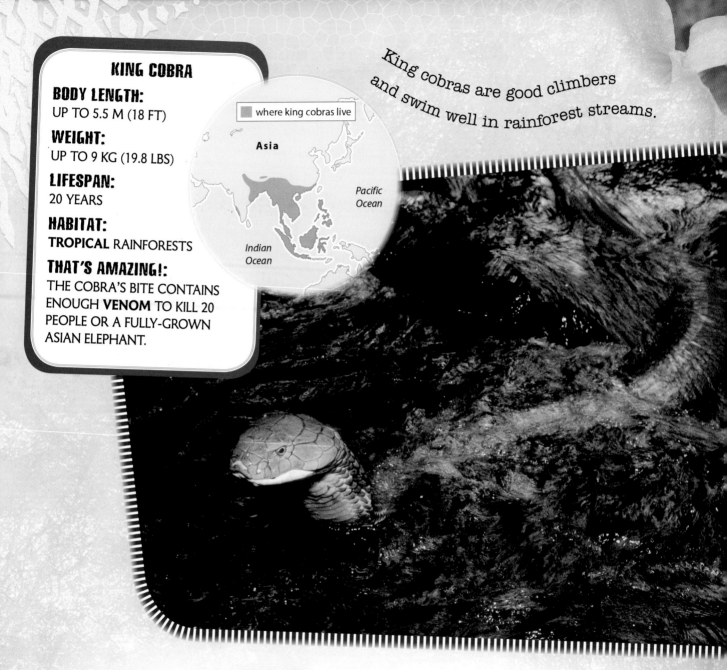

KING COBRA

BODY LENGTH:
UP TO 5.5 M (18 FT)

WEIGHT:
UP TO 9 KG (19.8 LBS)

LIFESPAN:
20 YEARS

HABITAT:
TROPICAL RAINFORESTS

THAT'S AMAZING!:
THE COBRA'S BITE CONTAINS ENOUGH **VENOM** TO KILL 20 PEOPLE OR A FULLY-GROWN ASIAN ELEPHANT.

where king cobras live

Asia

Pacific Ocean

Indian Ocean

King cobras are good climbers and swim well in rainforest streams.

Attack and defence

The king cobra eats other forest snakes. It kills its **prey** with a poisonous bite, then swallows it whole. The cobra also uses its poison in self defence. But first it tries to scare off its enemies by rearing up and spreading out the 'hood' of skin around its neck. If this does not work, the snake strikes.

Komodo dragon

The Komodo dragon is the largest lizard in the world. It is only found on the island of Komodo and a few other small islands in Indonesia. The dragon has a heavy body with thick legs and a long, muscular tail.

KOMODO DRAGON

BODY LENGTH:
UP TO 3 M (9.8 FT)

WEIGHT:
UP TO 90 KG (198 LBS)

LIFESPAN:
OVER 50 YEARS

HABITAT:
GRASSLANDS

THAT'S AMAZING!:
YOUNG KOMODO DRAGONS SPEND THEIR FIRST FOUR YEARS UP IN THE TREES, TO KEEP THEM SAFE FROM HUNGRY ADULTS.

where komodo dragons live

Asia

Pacific Ocean

Indian Ocean

The dragon's grey-brown skin keeps it **camouflaged** in the grasslands where it lives.

Some island animals, such as the Komodo dragon, grow to an enormous size. This is because islands are cut off from the mainland so there are fewer animals to compete for food. The Komodo dragon is the top **predator** in its **habitat** and top of the **food chain**.

A Komodo dragon can run fast after prey. It is also a good swimmer and climber.

Meat-eaters

Komodo dragons eat wild pigs, goats, and deer. They use their long, forked tongues to smell their **prey**. Then they grab it with their sharp claws, and bite off large chunks of flesh with their sharp, jagged teeth.

Yak

Yaks live in the mountains of northern India, Nepal, and China. They live higher up than any other **mammal**. When they are searching for food they reach heights of over 6,000 metres (19,680 feet).

YAK

HEIGHT AT SHOULDER:
OVER 2 M (6.5 FT)

WEIGHT:
UP TO 1 TONNE (1.1 TONS)

LIFESPAN:
OVER 20 YEARS

HABITAT:
MOUNTAINS

THAT'S AMAZING!:
YAKS TRAVEL ACROSS THE SNOW IN SINGLE FILE, CAREFULLY STEPPING INTO THE FOOTPRINTS MADE BY THE LEADING YAK.

In winter, yaks eat ice or snow to get water.

Peak survival

The weather conditions are difficult in the mountains, with freezing cold and howling winds. Yaks are very well **adapted** to their **habitat**. They have long, thick coats that reach almost down to the ground. Yaks graze on grass, lichens, and other plants. Because plants are scarce in the mountains, yaks have to travel long distances to feed. They are good climbers and can clamber over rough and icy ground.

Yaks' coats keep them warm in temperatures as low as -50°C (-58°F).

Giant panda

Giant pandas are large, heavy **mammals**. They live in **bamboo** forests on the slopes of a few mountains in south-west China. Giant pandas have black and white fur coats. Their fur is thick and waterproof to keep them warm and dry in their damp, cold **habitat**.

Giant panda cubs stay with their mothers for up to three years.

GIANT PANDA

BODY LENGTH:
1.6–1.9 M
(5.2–6.2 FT)

WEIGHT:
70–125 KG
(154–275 LBS)

LIFESPAN:
25–30 YEARS

HABITAT:
MOUNTAIN FORESTS

THAT'S AMAZING!:
A GIANT PANDA HAS A SPECIALLY **ADAPTED** WRIST BONE WHICH IT CAN USE LIKE A THUMB FOR GRIPPING STALKS OF BAMBOO.

where pandas live

Asia

Pacific Ocean

Indian Ocean

Bamboo diet

Giant pandas eat bamboo leaves and shoots and not much else. Pandas need to eat around 12.5 kilogrammes (27.6 pounds) a day to fill up. This means that they eat for up to 16 hours each day. Because they mainly eat one thing, pandas are very sensitive to changes in their habitat. If the bamboo dies or is cut down, the pandas die because there is nothing else for them to eat.

Bactrian camel

The two-humped Bactrian camel lives in the rocky **deserts** of central and eastern Asia. Here, the temperature can be baking hot in summer but bitterly cold in winter.

BACTRIAN CAMEL

HEIGHT AT HUMP:
OVER 2 M (6.5 FT)

WEIGHT:
OVER 725 KG (1,595 LBS)

LIFESPAN:
UP TO 50 YEARS

HABITAT:
DESERT

THAT'S AMAZING!:
A VERY THIRSTY CAMEL CAN DRINK AN AMAZING 135 LITRES (35.6 GALLONS) OF WATER IN JUST 13 MINUTES.

where Bactrian camels live

Asia

Pacific Ocean

Indian Ocean

This Bactrian camel still has its warm, winter coat.

These Bactrian camels are in their summer coats. They feed on thorny desert plants.

Desert features

The camel has many special features which help it to live in the desert. Its thick coat keeps it warm in winter but gets thinner in the warmer months. It has wide, flat feet for walking over the sand without sinking, and can close its nostrils to keep sand out. Bushy eyebrows and two rows of long eyelashes protect its eyes. The camel stores fat in its two humps. It can change the fat into water and energy. This means the camel can survive for several weeks without water or food.

Japanese giant salamander

The Japanese giant salamander is one of the world's biggest **amphibians**. It lives in cold, fast-flowing mountain rivers and streams in Japan. Its brown and black skin helps to hide it among the mud, stones, and plants. Amphibians can breathe through their skin. The salamander's skin takes in oxygen so that the salamander can breathe underwater.

The salamander uses its long, wide body and tail for swimming along the stream bed.

GIANT SALAMANDER

BODY LENGTH:
1.5 M (4.9 FT)

WEIGHT:
UP TO 25 KG (55 LBS)

LIFESPAN:
UP TO 50 YEARS

HABITAT:
RIVERS AND STREAMS

THAT'S AMAZING!:
WHEN A GIANT
SALAMANDER FEELS
THREATENED, IT OOZES OUT
A STICKY, SMELLY SUBSTANCE
FROM ITS SKIN.

where Japanese giant salamanders live

Asia

Pacific Ocean

Indian Ocean

Salamanders feed on fish, crabs, worms, and insects.

Salamander lifestyle

Giant salamanders spend the day sleeping underneath rocks. They look for food at night. They have tiny eyes on top of their heads and cannot see very well. Instead, they use smell and touch to find their way around and to find **prey**. They catch their prey with a quick snap of their large mouths.

Mudskipper

The mudskipper is a fish that can live partly out of the water. This allows it to feed on the many insects and shellfish in muddy mangrove **swamps**.

MUDSKIPPER

BODY LENGTH:
UP TO 20 CM (7.8 IN)

WEIGHT:
10–100 G (0.3–3.5 OZ)

LIFESPAN:
5 YEARS

HABITAT:
MANGROVE SWAMPS

THAT'S AMAZING!:
SOME MUDSKIPPERS BUILD MUD WALLS TO KEEP INTRUDERS OUT OF THEIR **TERRITORIES**.

where mudskippers live

Asia

Pacific Ocean

Indian Ocean

A mudskipper's bulging eyes are adapted for seeing both above and below water.

Mangrove swamps
Mangrove swamps grow along **tropical** coasts. They are named after the mangrove trees that stand in the mud on stilt-like roots. The swamps are used by many kinds of fish, **reptiles,** and birds as places to raise their young.

Life on the mud

Mudskippers are **adapted** to move on land. By flicking its tail, a fish can 'skip' across the mud. It can also use its front fins as legs. Fish normally use their **gills** to breathe oxygen from the water. On land, mudskippers keep their gill chambers full of water. They can also breathe through their skin as long as it is kept damp.

A mudskipper 'skipping' across the mud.

Animals in danger

Many animals in Asia are in danger of dying out. When an animal dies out, it is said to be **extinct**. Many animals are dying out because people are destroying their **habitats**, capturing them for pets, or killing them for their skins, meat, and body parts.

With its thick fur coat, and furry feet and tail, the snow leopard is **adapted** for surviving in its cold habitat. Its coat's black markings and whitish-grey colour help to **camouflage** it as it hunts its **prey**. Today, there may only be a few thousand snow leopards left because so many have been killed for their fur.

The snow leopard lives among the mountains of central Asia.

The Baikal seal is one of a few seals that live in freshwater.

Lake Baikal in Russia is home to the Baikal seal. Recently, the number of seals has been falling because thousands are hunted each year for their fur, meat, and oil. Their lake habitat is also under threat. Chemicals from factories and power stations around the lake are **polluting** the water. These chemicals can make the seals sick and stop them from breeding.

Today, **conservation** groups are working hard to save these amazing animals.

Animal facts and figures

There are millions of different kinds of animals living all over the world. The place where an animal lives is called its **habitat**. Animals have special features, such as wings, claws, and fins. These features allow animals to survive in their habitats. Which animal do you think is the most amazing?

BENGAL TIGER

BODY LENGTH:
2–3 M (8–10 FT)

WEIGHT:
100–300 KG (220–650 LBS)

LIFESPAN:
15 YEARS

HABITAT:
WOODLAND, **RAINFOREST**, MANGROVE **SWAMP**

THAT'S AMAZING!:
EACH TIGER'S STRIPES ARE DIFFERENT, JUST LIKE EACH PERSON'S FINGERPRINTS ARE DIFFERENT.

ORANG UTAN

BODY LENGTH:
1.3–1.8 M (4.2–5.9 FT)

WEIGHT:
35–80 KG (77–176 LBS)

LIFESPAN:
30–40 YEARS

HABITAT:
TROPICAL RAINFORESTS

THAT'S AMAZING!:
ORANG UTANS ARE ONE OF FOUR KINDS OF GREAT APES. THE OTHER THREE ARE GORILLAS, CHIMPANZEES AND BONOBOS.

GIANT ATLAS MOTH

BODY LENGTH:
OVER 8 CM (3.1 IN)

WINGSPAN:
25–30 CM (9.7–11.7 IN)

WEIGHT:
OVER 12 G (0.4 OZ)

LIFESPAN:
1–2 YEARS

HABITAT:
TROPICAL RAINFORESTS

THAT'S AMAZING!:
THE ATLAS MOTH IS NAMED AFTER THE MAP-LIKE MARKINGS ON ITS HUGE WINGS (AN ATLAS IS A BOOK OF MAPS).

KING COBRA

BODY LENGTH:
UP TO 5.5 M (18 FT)

WEIGHT:
UP TO 9 KG (19.8 LBS)

LIFESPAN:
20 YEARS

HABITAT:
TROPICAL RAINFORESTS

THAT'S AMAZING!:
THE COBRA'S BITE CONTAINS ENOUGH **VENOM** TO KILL 20 PEOPLE OR A FULLY-GROWN ASIAN ELEPHANT.

KOMODO DRAGON

BODY LENGTH:
UP TO 3 M (9.8 FT)

WEIGHT:
UP TO 90 KG (198 LBS)

LIFESPAN:
OVER 50 YEARS

HABITAT:
GRASSLANDS

THAT'S AMAZING!:
YOUNG KOMODO DRAGONS SPEND THEIR FIRST FOUR YEARS UP IN THE TREES, TO KEEP THEM SAFE FROM HUNGRY ADULTS.

YAK

HEIGHT AT SHOULDER:
OVER 2 M (6.5 FT)

WEIGHT:
UP TO 1 TONNE (1.1 TONS)

LIFESPAN:
OVER 20 YEARS

HABITAT:
MOUNTAINS

THAT'S AMAZING!:
YAKS TRAVEL ACROSS THE SNOW IN SINGLE FILE, CAREFULLY STEPPING INTO THE FOOTPRINTS MADE BY THE LEADING YAK.

GIANT PANDA

BODY LENGTH:
1.6–1.9 M (5.2–6.2 FT)

WEIGHT:
70–125 KG (154–275 LBS)

LIFESPAN:
25–30 YEARS

HABITAT:
MOUNTAIN FORESTS

THAT'S AMAZING!:
A GIANT PANDA HAS A SPECIALLY **ADAPTED** WRIST BONE WHICH IT CAN USE LIKE A THUMB FOR GRIPPING STALKS OF **BAMBOO**.

BACTRIAN CAMEL

HEIGHT AT HUMP:
OVER 2 M (6.5 FT)

WEIGHT:
OVER 725 KG (1,595 LBS)

LIFESPAN:
UP TO 50 YEARS

HABITAT:
DESERT

THAT'S AMAZING!:
A VERY THIRSTY CAMEL CAN DRINK AN AMAZING 135 LITRES (35.6 GALLONS) OF WATER IN JUST 13 MINUTES.

GIANT SALAMANDER

BODY LENGTH:
1.5 M (4.9 FT)

WEIGHT:
UP TO 25 KG (55 LBS)

LIFESPAN:
UP TO 50 YEARS

HABITAT:
RIVERS AND STREAMS

THAT'S AMAZING!:
WHEN A GIANT SALAMANDER FEELS THREATENED, IT OOZES OUT A STICKY, SMELLY SUBSTANCE FROM ITS SKIN.

MUDSKIPPER

BODY LENGTH:
UP TO 20 CM (7.8 IN)

WEIGHT:
10–100 G (0.3–3.5 OZ)

LIFESPAN:
5 YEARS

HABITAT:
MANGROVE SWAMPS

THAT'S AMAZING!:
SOME MUDSKIPPERS BUILD MUD WALLS TO KEEP INTRUDERS OUT OF THEIR **TERRITORIES**.

Find out more

Books to read

Exploring Continents: Asia, Anita Ganeri (Heinemann Library, 2007)

Living Things: Adaptation, Holly Wallace (Heinemann Library, 2001)

Living Things: Survival and Change, Holly Wallace (Heinemann Library, 2001)

Websites

http://www.bbc.co.uk/nature/reallywild
Type in the name of the animal you want to learn about and find a page with lots of facts, figures, and pictures.

http://animals.nationalgeographic.com/animals
This site has information on the different groups of animals, stories of survival in different habitats, and stunning photo galleries to search through.

http://animaldiversity.ummz.umich.edu
A website run by the University of Michigan which has a huge encyclopedia of animals to search through.

http://www.mnh.si.edu
The website of the Smithsonian National Museum of Natural History, which has one of the largest natural history collections in the world.

Zoo sites
Many zoos around the world have their own websites which tell you about the animals they keep, where they come from, and how they are looked after.

Glossary

adapted when an animal has special features that help it to survive in its habitat

amphibian animal, such as a toad or frog, that lives both on land and in the water

antennae feathery feelers on an insect's head which help it to pick up smells from the air

bamboo fast-growing kind of grass

camouflage when an animal has special colours or markings which help to hide it in its habitat

conservation saving and protecting wild animals and their habitats

desert dry, sandy region

equator imaginary horizontal line running around the middle of the Earth

extinct when a kind of animal dies out forever

food chain way in which animals are linked by what they eat

gill part of a fish's body that is used for breathing in the water

grassland huge, open space covered in grass and bushes

habitat place where an animal lives and feeds

mammal animal that has fur or hair and feeds its babies on milk

mate when an animal makes babies with another animal

pollution waste, litter, and spilt oil that makes a place dirty and unfit to live in

predator animal that hunts and kills other animals for food

prey animal that is hunted and killed by other animals for food

rainforest thick forest growing around the equator where the weather is hot and wet

reptile animal with scaly skin that lays eggs on land

swamp area where large parts of the land are usually or always under water

territory area where an animal or group of animals lives and feeds

tropical places around the equator which are hot and wet all year round

venom another word for poison

Index